Confessions

Confessions

Poems
by
Marcus Reichert

ZIGGURAT BOOKS
International

Confessions: Poems by Marcus Reichert
Copyright © 2010 by Marcus Reichert
Illustrations Copyright © 2010 by Marcus Reichert

All rights reserved. Except for brief passages quoted in a newspaper, magazine, radio, or television program, no part of this book may be reproduced in any form or by any means, electronic or mechanical, including photocopying and recording, or by any information storage and retrieval system, without permission in writing from the Publisher.

Front cover painting:
Figure in the Street 2007 by Marcus Reichert
Back cover portrait of the author by Edward Rozzo

UK office: 27 St. Quentin House, Fitzhugh Grove,
London SW18 3SE, England
Editorial office: 6 rue Argenterie,
30170 St. Hippolyte du Fort, France
Enquiries: zigguratbooks@orange.fr

Printed by Imprint Digital, Upton Pyne, Exeter

Distributed by Central Books Ltd.
99 Wallis Road, London E9 5LN, England
Tel UK: 0845 458 9911
Fax UK: 0845 459 9912
Tel International: +44 20 8525 8800
Fax International: +44 20 8525 8879
E-mail: orders@centralbooks.com

First Edition

ISBN 978-0-9566579-1-6

Marcus Reichert is a painter and a poet who has also worked in film. His film works are held in the Archive of the Museum of Modern Art, New York. *Reichert: The Human Edifice* by Mel Gooding, with 100 photographs by the artist in colour, is published by Artmedia Press, London. *Displaced Person: Poetry, Pornography & Politics* (Selected Writings 1970-2005) and *Art & Ego: Marcus Reichert in Conversation with Edward Rozzo* (2007) are published by Ziggurat Books, London & Paris. Marcus Reichert is the author of three novels: *Verdon Angster*, *The Miracle of Fontana's Monkey*, and *Hoboken*. He lives and works in the south of France.

Donald Kuspit is one of America's most distinguished art critics and a poet. He is Distinguished Professor of Art History and Philosophy at the State University of New York at Stony Brook. Professor Kuspit is a Contributing Editor at *Artforum*, *Sculpture*, and *Tema Celeste* magazines, and the editor of *Art Criticism*. Among Donald Kuspit's most recent books are *Psychostrategies of Avant-Garde Art* (New York: Cambridge University Press, 2000) and *The End of Art* (New York: Cambridge University Press, 2004). He is also the author of four books of poetry: *Self-Refraction* (1983; visual accompaniment by Rudolf Baranik); *Apocalypse with Jewels in the Distance* (2000; visual accompaniment by Rosalind Schwartz); *On The Gathering Emptiness* (2004; visual accompaniment by Walter Feldman and Hans Breder); and *The Gods and Other Beings* (2010).

Contents

Introduction
by Donald Kuspit 1

I.

We Live Our Lives 5

Normal Flesh 6

In This Place 8

Eden Falls 9

Mother Sorrow 10

Tell Me Something 11

Send Me No Light 12

The Summer Is Gone 13

No One Should 14

River With No Name 15

Sweet Healing Hands 16

Light Of Day 18

To Suffer The Magnitude 19

Your Hatred 20

The Supplicant's Palms 21

Is My Father Waiting 22

My Brother Lies Somewhere 23

Do You Really 24

My Casual Heart 25

On Dying 27

II.

Not Breathing 31

No Soldier 32

Like A Mockingbird 33

Disembodiment And Fracture 34

Corrupted Instinct 36

Creatures In The Street 38

Their Bodies 39

As The Heavens Fall 40

Dreaded City 42

Within This Confine 45

The Fire 46

She Was 47

Blacker Still 48

A Man Is Waiting 49

Destitute Saint 50

To Subdue The Wounded Beast 51

Magnum Dictum 53

The Sublime Creation 55

Afterword

Suspended in Doubt:
Notes on the Deluge of Thought 57

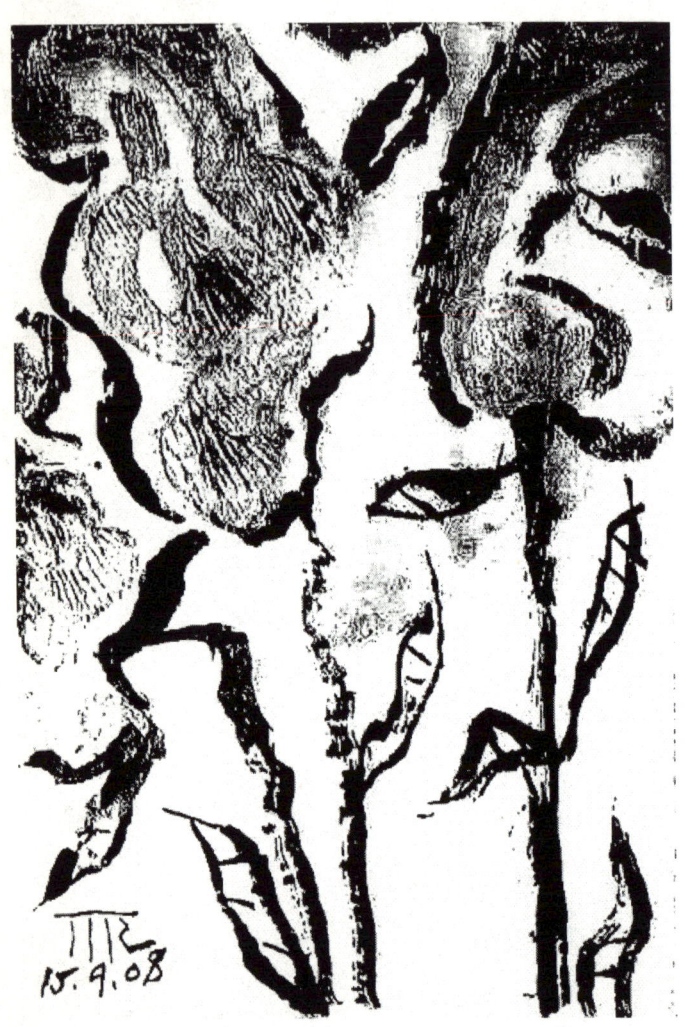

Introduction

Introduction
by Donald Kuspit

Marcus Reichert's *Confessions* are morbidly personal, obsessed with death – of loved ones, of the body battered by time and experience – but trumping it with a certain reflectiveness, as though viewing it from a philosophical distance, allowing him to accept its inevitability. The poems are accompanied by gestural paintings of black knots, pictorially the "collapsing flower" referred to in one poem, more pointedly emblems of the poems' "abject euphoria," to refer to another poignant phrase. There are no moments of unlived life in Reichert's poems, or of life unconscious of itself: he has made the flesh of impassioned suffering insinuating language. He offers us a Heracleitean stream of self-reflection into which we can step more than once, for we can see ourselves empathically mirrored in it: Reichert's interiority is our own.

I.

WE LIVE OUR LIVES

We live our lives as we choose,
here on the street, without pride
or grievance, or longing for much.
We drink our drinks and smoke,
we say only what we must, or
what we will, in our abject euphoria.
The sun shines and the wind blows,
cars pass beyond a distant window,
legs adjust, feet stop and start.
Someone just spoke to me, but
I don't know what he said, only,
conceivably, what he didn't.
His face in profile is the face of
a ruined king, a lachrymose cardinal.
Now when he turns to me, if he does,
I will know him utterly as himself,
without his work, without his wife,
without his children, or his dead father.
His mother is beckoning from the hill,
calling silently for him to make her meal;
these are the things they've grown
in the garden they share with their God.
Their God speaks through this man
in mute testimony to all that is unknown
to me and will never be known to me –
here in this bar, in this sweet purgatory
of unnumbered days and evenings.

NORMAL FLESH

Normal flesh
is not old flesh,
but old flesh
is normal flesh.

The ring of the neck
subsides,
the stem of the flower
collapsing,
the ardent rain
gathering
in puddles of forgetting.

The belly as it plunges
recalls the upended
buoyancy of the ego,
now a song of the flesh
without substance,
without responsibility,
or lusting ambition.

As memory retreats
within the flesh,
sentiment recoils in defeat,
knowing nothing but
the wanton aggression
and infantile appetites
of reality's wicked plan.

Once we knew the flesh's
urgent need to replace itself,
to submerge itself
in other flesh,
to selfishly sacrifice
itself to itself,
to its *own* infantile appetites.

Normal flesh
is the old flesh
that reality consumes
without concession,
or gratitude, or remorse.

IN THIS PLACE

Almost every day here is wonderfully sunny.
Some people think it's good to be in a place
like this at the end of your life. The thing is,
it's sad to be in a place like this when it's
not the end of your life. The days are only
as long as the day is long and the nights are
the eternity that we were never meant to know.

EDEN FALLS

Eden falls with the summer leaves,
steadily shaken by the lethargic tumult
of our innumerable transgressions,
nothing left but unreliable sentiment
in the wake of our grand devouring.

What is there to feed on but regret,
what exotic beast can escape our hunger?
Tables are strewn like countless rich islands
over the banquet floor, a sea without shores,
a garden made for disorientated beings.

Insinuating itself in our midst is the need
to think things through after the brutal fact
of our ludicrous self-indulgence, our pride
kept intact by the residual sampling of treats –
now, abundantly full, we drink of our souls.

My house is your house is his house is mine,
and the towers rise from every skewed corner
as the windows erupt with cold artificial light.
Assume you know nothing when you step inside,
assume you know only of our shared goodness.

Herewith, the charter we've written with tickets
attached for the many who would seek our vision,
a vision without a single flaw, painstakingly true
to the hybrid form we were handed by strategists,
geniuses who fed upon no earthly flesh, only light.

At dusk, we watch our children leave the hollow,
unaware in our communion with ourselves that
they could find nothing, no refuge in the sublime
moments past. They beckon from afar, the gates
closed permanently behind them, like eyelids.

MOTHER SORROW

Faces shine forth in the night and emancipate us
from our dread. Our bodies swarm towards
each other in dreaming aberration, and in mute
immediate joy in the street without calculation.
The totality of our experience is our love,
until sorrow brings us down into ourselves,
without favour or fear, only the murmuring
of our unspent joy, then silence one to the next.
The wind drifts across our lips, and drink fills
our hearts with longing and nothingness as
swallows swoop and fall, heavenly spirits undone.

My worldly pose was lost to despair when a man,
unknown to me but darkly familiar, said:

*My life and love are broken, my mother took me,
left me here forever broken and ugly and unworthy.*

And I said:

*Let this river take us down, down into the emptiness
that is ours, our destitute and yearning souls unknown
to a mother's love, theirs lost to a child's sacrifice.
From the bottom of this river we shall look up and
together see the vast beauty of this night, our night.*

Occasionally, the street brings this man to me and it is
always a new moment beyond that other world of pain
and humiliation we have forsaken between ourselves.

TELL ME SOMETHING

What would she say,
at the end of this long evening,
among the dead to be dead?

Tell me something of their despair,
tell me something of their remorse,
tell me what they need to do to love,
tell me what I need to know to love.

Oh sweet gate,
cry for me.
Oh cigarette smoke,
make do for me.
Oh sweet heaven,
take this child lost in me.

Swooping down now,
the sound of the flood
coming swiftly to take me
as I awaken into the words
that are hers and, together,
we gratefully say good-bye.

SEND ME NO LIGHT

Send me no light
on these winnowing hills
to drive me
deeper into chaos.

Please do not lead me
down into her valleys,
as she tells me
the untruths of centuries.

Please do not break
this infernal calm
with the sound
of grasses heaving
in a succulent wind.

Please allow me
no passage,
only the isolation
of those souls undone by
this vision of the river:

The hills shall take you down
to the light of the river and,
once there, you shall drown
in the sweet currents of your joy.

THE SUMMER IS GONE

The summer is gone, lost in the wake
of my torments, rain falling through
these streets to wet the tongues
of the war dead, their spirits infusing
my thoughts as with each breath
the winds of fire lay the sedentary
to waste with my memories of what
I was before the pain of endless hours
unhinged me, before I knew nothing.

I look to the body of my wife
for respite from the broken years
that have sped beyond the frame
of her endurance and mine;
the flowers that however endure
within her are mine to breathe
as we are guided by ill-fortune
to the everlasting summit of our
exalted weariness and insoluble joy.

The rain brings these errant fires to rest,
it melts over the tomb of life's aberration
as the tides of our merging seas bear
no untruths and silently withdraw from
any reality known in faith or fantasy.
We are left in a peace unknown to
us before, here within the sanctity of
our devotion, now only dimly encumbered
by a distant belief in time and memory.

NO ONE SHOULD

No one should suffer:
it is beyond reason.
No not a child,
no not an old person,
no not you or me.
Life makes nothing
heroic of itself
when we suffer.

Now the cold towel
comes down on
the forehead and
our thoughts retreat
into the shadows
as we are subdued
by the beauty that
once consumed us.

RIVER WITH NO NAME

My guts are wracked with pain,
the drugs only capable of losing
themselves inside me like mush.
No doctor touches my hand, only
my wife who knows that to touch
is, in such circumstances, to disown.
I once was on a river and that river
made no sense because it was a river
with a name. The river in which you
will watch me dissolve has no name.
I shall look for the remnants of hope
in the depths of that river, my love
nonsensically wanting for me to be
saved and for this bed to float away.

SWEET HEALING HANDS

Sweet healing hands,
dear lover's hands,
take me through
to heaven.

The world outside
now releases itself
as the source of the river
is lost in the sea.

Sweet soothing lips,
dear breasts on fire,
burn away this pain
forever.

The world outside
now embraces itself
as the source of the river
is lost in my soul.

Sweet endearing eyes,
dear breath of life
breathe into me
only yourself.

The world outside
now forgets us both
but no harm shall come
to our sailing hearts.

Sweet emerging love,
dear lives untold,
sweep me up
in your starry night.

The world outside
now is only darkness
as the light has gone,
but not from you.

LIGHT OF DAY

What is the sky telling us tonight,
deeper and darker than a mother's breath?
No dimension to hold us to our thoughts,
our thoughts scatter solemnly, wanting
to feel the stars mingle with them.
The flutes, in resonant harmony, are
nothing if not light, our foreboding
rendered askew. Adoration of the saints
harbours within us, as if we were motors
running on rarefied blood. We endure
the haphazard articulation of life's design,
shedding abundant tears filled with song,
the injured heart healing itself, yearning
for the night to be done and pale dawn
to bring the emancipating light of day.

TO SUFFER THE MAGNITUDE

To suffer the magnitude
of discipline is to suffer
no beliefs or childish whims,
but to envisage the ruination
of all men in the throes
of their enforced undoing.

I creep into the crevices
of my aggrieved soul unleashing
the broken glass and ash
of a million destroyed homes,
my children running terrified
from the cry of my voice.

Dogs follow me in the street,
they can smell the fear on me,
the bad blood rising in my veins.
The warm tea turns to vomit,
it takes them by their snouts,
it wrenches them backwards.

Mother's hand across my face,
father's absence a disgrace,
the quiet that lies within these walls
summons the monsters of oblivion
for humanity and its craven images,
for discreet lying tongues eternal.

YOUR HATRED

Your hatred, in its violence,
hammers at the chambers
of my heart, as down I tumble,
limbs trembling with anger
at the implacable arrogance
of your ignorance, at the wilful
obliviousness of your gaze,
at your mute unflinching pride.

THE SUPPLICANT'S PALMS

Over the supplicant's palms
blow the slick breezes
of your empty words,
the compliant posture and
trembling fingers and tongue
of the benighted enriching
your rhetoric and your greed.

Succumb we must and be
grateful for your meagre
generosity, your omnipotence
our only beacon in the night.
Mindlessly, we drink down
the intoxicating gyrations
of your dwindling breasts.

I am exceedingly grateful
to be just another kneeling
at the edge of your lazy river,
its grandeur too magnificent
for this child to comprehend.
May I too be so bountiful
in the autumn of my years.

IS MY FATHER WAITING

Is my father waiting for my mother
in his grave,
does he speak to her as I speak
to him,
does he tell of the unknown love,
the impossible,
does he touch her as she
reaches for him
in her despair as her death approaches
and I stand here watching nothing
but them.

Take me with you as we never were,
as I always wanted to love you,
to find the beauty in what
you never found.

Perhaps one day you will find what I knew
you to be,
perhaps one day you will forgive each other
as I now forgive you.

Take me with you now unselfishly,
take me with you as you are joined,
take me with you as never before.

MY BROTHER LIES SOMEWHERE

My brother lies somewhere dying,
his face the face of the angel I knew,
a wicked angel abandoned at birth
by his own soul and life's undoing:
not anything, no not anything,
now haunted, now lost forever.

Take my child's body if it makes
you know what life might be,
but, please, leave my soul behind.
You have unknowingly taken this too,
because inside you, hiding, was love.
What no one once knew but me
they will never forgive you for,
but I will never forsake you:
nothing matters but our resolve,
for there shines the redeeming light.
We shall never again hurt anyone,
not each other, not another, no one,
for we are together in our despair.
No mother, no father, only you
and me up high in a dark place.
Take me to you, take me without
knowing any sort of reason why.
This child's love is unselfish as
naked I go from our warm room
into the whirling snow and night.

DO YOU REALLY

Do you really need to steal,
right from under her nose?
She'd gone to get her bottle
in the newspapers but you'd
hidden it somewhere else.
The time it takes to die
in the electric chair is
surely less time than it
takes to smoke one of your
mother's precious cigarettes.
Now you've been found out,
and so how do you feel?

They break our hearts, the dead,
stealing themselves from us as if
we'd never known they would go,
turning their smiles remotely
upon us in dreams, like light on
autumn leaves guiding the way
to nowhere and to nothingness,
the bliss that would signal
their return never to engage us
but for that last instant of love,
as we are stolen too, like slaves.

MY CASUAL HEART
On Religion

Fires burning to keep
the howling cold at bay,
St. Stephen's Day
draws to a close.
We assume the posture
of the drowsy
double-backed beast.
Yes, we shall hibernate
until the sun
creeps over the equator
and the skin
loosens pleasantly
with the promise
of nature's heat.

On the Day we drank
to your savage gods
but now we cower
at the thought
of their return.
May they never more,
especially in celebration,
be manifest
in my casual heart,
but together let us
only watch
as they come perpetually
to inhabit the countless
inelegant bodies
of the others
who writhe with dread
content.

Thankfully,
the gifts are all dispersed
and the eating
less mordantly abundant,
as now we retire
with the evening shadows
and so very,
very sweetly are embraced
by nothing more
ominous than sleep.

ON DYING

When we can no longer remember
our life unfolding with any vitality,
no beauty known beyond our own
deterioration, adrift in a static sea
of compliant malignancy, yearning
for the shifting detritus of summer
to smother the forest's pristine floor,
we are flowers burst into useless flame
upon the bed in which we were born.

He said, walk here with me and I did.
The street was not his alone, it was shared
by others, by mere mortals like myself.
Whosoever walks here is mine, he said,
and I shall have them utterly and completely.
Now my thoughts are beating, alive without
respite, as I endure the torment that is his —
mute flowers burst into flame, left to endure
the silence of loved ones awkwardly waiting.

The woman who takes me down into the
smouldering leaves of my thought also opens
the sky wide with redemption as I plainly see
the sympathy of others alone in their fear,
knowing they shall, like me, finally lie down
somewhere within the misbegotten vastness
that is the grandeur of our oblivion. Mingle
with me, she says, as we are taken beyond
the cinders of sun and moon to where we began.

II.

NOT BREATHING

Somewhere just this side of
dawn, he wakes up not breathing,
looks at the clock and thinks:
now, I've finally done something
without trying, without anyone
telling me to hurry up, or to wait,
while I take my time not getting
there, and it was easy as cream pie.
Remember how every day or so
a shadow would cross your path?
he asks himself, knowing no
shadow ever did, or spoke
to him, or showed him the way
down to the river where
everyone else makes love,
where everyone else finds
something to do that they
can't do in the light of day.
Except stop breathing, which
is now his strength, his pride,
award-winning as it isn't but
then, sudden as toast, he
gasps, taking in the air, and
it's all over, all that sweet
exclusivity is gone, and he's
walking along the dark river,
watching, after not working.

NO SOLDIER

Imagine if I had a bottle of whisky
to account for each lonely horror,
sunny streets unknown to men like me,
women's pretty faces disappearing
without ever saying good-bye or,
for that matter, ever knowing who
I ever was once.

Imagine if I had a lot of money
to spend at will, all of the mistakes
I would make benefitting new friends,
repairing my inadvertent transgressions,
trying my best to assume the stature
of a man who manages to live without
malice aforethought.

Imagine if I had known enough
to save myself, but I knew nothing
whatsoever, only lied to myself,
to my family and very dearest friend,
telling them of my love and determination
to bring myself home whole and just as
I was before.

LIKE A MOCKINGBIRD

She dances along not thinking
that she might fall down, down.
Oh my breasts, they'll keep me
afloat, she murmurs, and she
knows she looks so very good.
Where's my mom tonight? –
she frowns, knowing that she's
dead, and old Ralph, the bastard,
he's singing somewhere high up
in his tree like a mockingbird.
And still, how I loved him so,
because he brought the big love
into my room without anything
but tenderness, and never said
nothing bad about me or my
mom, no not never, and I
won't be like her, no not never.
I wouldn't let a fucker like
him get away, with so much
money and good looks too.

DISEMBODIMENT AND FRACTURE

Daffodils, paint me cut daffodils
reclining in a summer hat,
said the collector without irony,
tawny port colouring his mouth;
the kind of hat that might adorn
the head of a beautiful woman,
a gatherer of ephemera and dreams
whispering to herself, fear not me.

If I were to buy every painting you've painted,
what would I have to pay;
if I were to burn every painting you've painted,
how big a fire would it make?

The world turns on the pivoting of a coin,
and that coin is essentially without substance,
so says the painter, still lying to himself,
his hand languishing at the bottom of a well.
Munch had vanished from his mirror,
as had Beckmann, and Freida Kahlo;
only their teeth survived the winter,
hidden like harbour lights within a fog.

If I were to buy every painting you've painted,
what would I have to pay;
if I were to burn every painting you've painted,
how big a fire would it make?

Now, when you look at one of my paintings,
he said, nerve quivering round his left eye,
you are staring down the barrel of a loaded gun.
Beautiful, is it not, what with the face of a goat
looking eerily like a newsreader known to many?
Very soon I will be what they call a *talking head* –
a head without a body, surely without a mind,
an epitome of nonsensical elaboration, no more.

If I were to buy every painting you've painted,
what would I have to pay;
if I were to burn every painting you've painted,
how big a fire would it make?

CORRUPTED INSTINCT

Corrupted instinct stalks
the civilized animal
who knows no task
too great or too small
for his civilizing appetites.

In his car, he thinks on food,
on its derivations as they might
portend the suffering of others
less fortunate than food itself.

In his bathroom, he ponders
himself, and his significance
assumes new dimensions
of beatific identification.

In his wife, he finds real trust,
not the ambivalent sort but
the kind that endures beyond
reason, psychology, or science.

In his children, above all else,
he finds himself, the wonder
of romantic ages past, of giddy
heights and deplorable lows.

In his union with the fish,
he finds, against all odds,
the abstracted head of a goat,
a shoe that tells a tragic story.

In his seat at the ball park,
he breathes the sweet air,
he eats the salty piquant meats,
he plunders his sparkling pockets.

In his lugubrious joy and sorrow,
he recalls his mother's disdain,
his father's head in the rain,
a playmate's fist in his stomach.

Blithe currents of remembering
inflict their subtle tattoos upon
the rectified content of the brain
of the civilized animal as he now
lunges in sleep between two worlds.

CREATURES IN THE STREET

Shingles fall from his brow,
roof that covers the world.
Raising himself from his bed,
demanding nothing but sleep,
and still it goes on, the sorrow.
The creatures in the street,
who live without solace,
are harbouring within him,
awake or asleep, although
it very seldom gets that good.
And his mind knows no quiet,
but it is nothing as compared to
a heartfelt round of applause,
because he can't now recall
how his kindness shone, and
it's time to stop remembering.
Send me all those leftover
flowers, he says, from all those
things that were cancelled,
all those things that had to do
with sadness, with celebration,
with any kind of love whatsoever.
Just, please, send them to me
because I've got room here.

THEIR BODIES

Their bodies lie side by side,
their expressions lost to each other.
Only now do we know who they were,
only now do we care if they ever lived.
His hand in hers, hers in his, this is
the union that surpasses the madness
that brought them to this end.
He tells her now: I shall always love you.
And she responds: Even though.
The end that was theirs was no end whatsoever:
they walk away from our fuming eyes,
they walk away from everything that
brought them to this unspeakable end.
They walk away to love each other forever,
they walk away as we look on in horror.

AS THE HEAVENS FALL
On 9/11

As the heavens fall,
so too falls the hour.
The drafts of a thousand
empty rooms
dance over the streets,
then retreat.

Out of the fiery crease
they emerge,
seeking refuge from a storm
they cannot name,
while on their lips
trembles
the Word of God.

Nearer the sun,
others abandon themselves
into the light –
to fill their despairing souls
with the uplifting breath
of eternity.
And, as they fall,
delicate leaves
from silver birches,
we wonder.

From our balconies
we watch and
grow quieter still,
for now the wind,
once fragrant
with the scent
of the World's glory
and its decay,
blows through
our hearts too.

Like the desiccated moss
that once adorned
the weary flanks
of Brother Tommaso's tomb,
the weakening fibre of hope
shimmers with
the sun's healing rays
and turns to dust.

Today we weep
for the unnamed joy.

DREADED CITY
War in the Streets of Baghdad

I.

As a city grows, like a wild fungus
in the mind, it also spirals into pockets
of the ether, reaches up to haul down
the stars, and drive them into man's
nocturnal repositories – bars and discos,
cinemas, cafeterias, living-rooms, even
churches – for cities are beyond the
imagination, beyond the confines of
military strategy and its contingencies.
No army can penetrate the city's psyche,
neither can any mortal force destroy it;
the myriad souls who comprise its fabric
do not question the motives of the intruder,
for they instinctively know he has come
to violate and undo, to at least humiliate.

Those who, day after day, walk its streets,
smell its seasons changing, survive amidst
the city's complex of prejudices, accepting
the selfless inevitability of compromise,
reject and deny the invaders' alien logic.
These, the conqueror thinks, are the sorry,
uncivilized souls who have been waiting
to be embraced by my wealth, wanting
merely to walk shoulder-to-shoulder with
our legions, beneficent liberators all.
But the city waits to pop this fantasy
hungrily into its mouth, like a fat grape.

II.

His house blown to bits, wife and
children dead, a man is determined
to punish, at any cost, those
responsible. Out of the shattered
doorway emerges his ghastly
spectre, no onslaught equal to his
appetite for revenge. The streets
in which he played as a child are
now a jungle of fractured memories.

The soldier, trapped in a maze
of indecipherable signage,
corridors of shadow and light
signifying his mortality, hears
his brain stammer: lost but for
my weapon. How far the conqueror
travels, each city a wedding cake
on the horizon, a hornets' nest
fallen from a limb of purple cloud.

For the invader, there is nothing
more satisfying than marching
triumphantly along the enemy's
boulevards, and nothing more
anguishing for a city's people
to behold. The dance of liberation
is one without artifice, essential to
the resurrection of heartache.

Missiles ripping through steel
and concrete, shrapnel shattering
windows, penetrating flimsy
bathroom walls, abject fear
pervades the subconscious
to harvest depression and
psychosis, often eternally so.

Out of the desert mists, the tanks
lumber in, buildings reduced to
rubble. No semblance of a society
remains to hold aloft courageous
thoughts unfolding, only bitterness
driving bleak ingenuity into
each darkened crevice. Women
eventually appear, wanting for sanity.

The older men imprisoned or dead,
boys barely in their teens are left
to face the occupying forces.
For years to come, these young men
will scrub clean their streets with
the blood of unsuspecting soldiers.
And the memory of each dead
soldier's friendly disposition and
unseemly largesse will bring a smile
to brighten each young man's face.

WITHIN THIS CONFINE

Within this confine
lies the misbegotten,
never to adore,
never to comprehend,
never to hold
the treasures known
to another.

Within this confine
lies the enraptured,
never to dismiss,
never to mistreat,
never to question
the love given
by another.

Within this confine
lies the serpent,
never to strike,
never to entangle,
never to squeeze
the breath of life
from another.

THE FIRE

Let me hear you,
let me see you,
don't let me be
the last one out.

SHE WAS

She was
dead for
a long time:
the cat ate
her tongue
before they
found her.

BLACKER STILL

His huge prick lies in
the hands of the authorities
holding him prisoner,
as the women's teeth
turn black, but their lips
turn blacker still.

"We are all getting
older by the minute,"
says the huge prick.
"And we are all
getting harder," say
the police as one,
as the women's teeth
turn black, but their lips
turn blacker still.

"Time can't possibly
heal this wound,"
says the huge prick.
"Neither are we doctors,
nor nurses," say the men
with the women's black
teeth in their hands,
and the women's black lips
fastened round their knobs.

"Oh, now I understand,"
says the huge prick,
wanting for nothing but mercy.
"No, you don't," say the cops,
their lips and teeth now turning
blacker than death warmed over.

A MAN IS WAITING

Now bump and grind,
now horsewhip your minions,
now make the Chinese pay
for all of the wrong that
little shits have done you.
Basically, she says, everyone
gets fucked in life but learns
to like it, even a lot, yes please.

If we were to suppose, she goes on,
that nearly everything is honky dory
from the outset then there wouldn't be
much interest in just about anything.
Now, rise up on your toes, she says,
and show me the tip of your tongue
as we fornicate myself into the higher
regions of heavenly bliss, yes please.

Downstairs, a man is waiting,
cap and money in hand, but
never once does he think about
what might be going on in No.12.
The man downstairs only thinks
of Jesus Christ, who had lain
on his slab of stone knowing
everything that he, the man,
would never come to know.

DESTITUTE SAINT

Demons beware,
the vessel is broken;
the haunted man,
once sought not found,
is now among us.
Who shall comprehend
the silence of him,
he who speaks within,
as without the silence
blisters?

"Rejoice in me," he murmurs,
"hear what has never been
said before or be doomed
to the mute unedifying
indulgences of the womb."

They come, his followers,
to embrace his thoughts,
the exalted who know
nothing of this world;
these are the adoring ones,
their innocence immemorial,
children who sing not of salvation,
nor of the healing waters,
but only of a contentment unbounded,
of the exquisite unbridled hours spent
waiting for him to return.

TO SUBDUE THE WOUNDED BEAST

To subdue the wounded beast
is to die a thousand deaths
as the passage of time collapses
with each dying breath
and these mediocre clichés abound.

The winds of despair sail high,
up, up into the grinning mouth
of easy opportunity and shame,
as regret's unidentified cargo
is left mouldering on the dock.

The single most obdurate being
finds comfort in the meagre remains
of a life not worth knowing,
although within one life adheres
the minutiae of loss and profit.

The angels on high sing in unison
of the annihilation of unbridled thought,
paradoxically without avenging malice,
alert to the slightest empirical movement
of the retreating mind and destitute soul.

Cars pass in the street like snails,
the fuel that informs their thoughts
harvested continuously in empty gardens
of artificial light and the resonating din
of the perilous unknown, still unknown.

Disembark, moans the stuperous conductor,
eyes watching for stray wife or daughter
amongst the crowd of bedraggled strangers,
their burdens suddenly made lighter
by the aroma of crackling electrodes.

The sweet schmoozy sofa awaits them,
broken in nicely by burgeoning buttocks
and rutting bludgeons of epic proportions,
but alas the tired plates of meat that flew
from the corner shop no affirmation make.

Saddled up and ready to roll in tow
are the missionary vessels of Eros himself,
his diminutive frame awakened with delight
as fantastic molten iron scalds the waves
of unrehearsed Christmases past and present.

Her name, he now recalls, was Susan,
and a childish name at that, in repose
not sophisticated like some but inert
and without the stature of the numinous few
who make all of the Susans pay beforehand.

Now he wanly gazes out upon the swans
as history endlessly repeats itself as itself,
a cauldron of seething lycra ready to ingest
the money that no uncle could possibly earn,
only his false teeth worth the price of admission.

Unbending, the beast alights like a fly
upon the gorgeous nose of trendy Medusa,
her mouth wrought askew with the stink
of her own demise, but nevertheless proud
of her sterling children now graded superbly.

Just think – to subdue the wounded beast
is to know the rigors of predetermination,
of absolution, of the hierarchies of success,
for within this glowing suite of rooms
resides the peace that is butter on toast.

MAGNUM DICTUM
The Viceroy's Siesta

Yes, my
id is a pid
in a pod,
that's me.

My magnum dictum,
like the accountant's
brief,
cloisters the thief,
as his id from its piddling
pod
descends to rivulet
the welcoming palms
of Misfortune
and her sister, Ilene.

Of vinegar and
saccharine
the two sing,
occasionally:

*How blue, how blue
the sea does shine
in our beguiling eyes,
as its vagrant mists
play upon our breasts,
yielding but resilient,
and we effortlessly
shift our dappled limbs
into position.*

Assault he must
the towering precipice
of his lobster salad
and digest before
commencing further.

In the afternoon,
Misfortune and Ilene
casually make use
of his rumoured
stamina, shredded
but not shaken.

After, he watches
Ilene in repose,
modest restraints
and musty drapes
of the confessional
eschewed,
while Misfortune
too reclines,
vertically behind
the diamond light
of the shower curtain,
his thirst momentarily
subdued
by Boticelli's palette.

And so, amidst his slumbers,
his pid once again alights
upon one tousled head still wet,
not Misfortune's but her sister's,
in a world without split-ends,
amen.

THE SUBLIME CREATION

The *sublime creation*,
as they prefer to be known,
appeared on the island
entranced by all that they saw.
Their appearance was evidently
a miracle without calculation.
When the tree faeries run,
they run from these monsters,
spoken of only in hushed tones.
The pious among these intruders
steadfastly nurture their sublimity,
but they are fools unto themselves,
lost in the lather of the moment
as their god – the magnificent
abstraction they call eternity –
drifts cruelly about them.

SUSPENDED IN DOUBT
Notes on the Deluge of Thought

Insidious, as it begins without being perceived on any level of consciousness. The swell of energy flows into the mind imperceptibly. The window is open, sunlight bathing the building across the way, the street below populated loosely by the occasional neighbour on his way to the market, a young couple pushing their baby on before them in a gondola of modern excellence. These are the sensations, both still and moving, that register on the psyche, but not the unknown configurations that will unleash themselves within the chambers of thought drowning all thought in a gleaming river of ecstasy, a confounding ecstasy that will only subside when its mute satisfaction has been realized. The deluge will leave its victim and the witnesses to his subjugation exhausted.

As the deluge progresses, a contrary stillness comes to dominate the centre of all reasoning. This occurs with such slow uncanny exactitude that what might be manifest at the time, be it via image or word, lives exclusively within its own logic. What unfolds before our eyes, rushing from the unknown source of this *inspiration*, can, at moments, altogether unpredictably belie our worst instincts. Ultimately, we strive to decipher a coherency in the spontaneity of our efforts, and the power of this tumultuous work becomes our sole preoccupation for hours on end.

On the canvas appears a flower that becomes a face that reminds us of someone, but that someone's presence lurks somewhere in the future, a future that exists only within that moment — when the flower became a face. The image is removed (physically eradicated with some unfeeling thing) as our consternation envelops us, another inevitable aspect of the deluge, and we begin again. Now, our determination somehow restored, we shall find something that we will secretly acknowledge to be outside the mendacious inadequacy of our usual comforting procedures. Now we shall accept, albeit in fleeting moments of reflection, that there is a governing force beyond the mundane ideas that in their essence deny the unpredictable evocations and metaphors that instinctively consume our thought. Out of the deluge unexpectedly rises an unashamed pleading for rectitude — our images, our words *must* have integrity.

Thought now is impulse. The banks of the river have disappeared. The water is rising to turgidly lap the shop fronts as the town's people watch anxiously from their balconies. There is an unknown excitement in the air, it hovers everywhere like vast swarms of mosquitoes. But no one sees us in our stillness, being swept along as if upon a buoyant chaise, our arms outstretched in anticipation of that phantom obstacle that never lunges up out of the relentless flow and into our path to destroy us. We simply move along helplessly empowered by the deluge's currents, in turns elevating and debilitating, momentarily ragged then limp. What we had once ingested, loaded with toxic aesthetics, is evacuated while we simultaneously gorge ourselves on the crystalline air that suddenly sweeps across every surface before us and into our emptying souls, as if an entire meal of abrogations — the unpalatable rules of someone else's game — were being swallowed whole. Now the flower becomes a face that we know, a face that we have known forever. And the face rapidly acquires a body and a disposition that is an extension of what we are seeking — the beginning of a way out.

In a room with words painstakingly making pages, while engaging paint and surface and obliquely glimpsing a configuration of gestures that isn't as yet itself, the dialogue faintly then more forcefully seeps in to dominate our thoughts. Whose voice is that? And we haven't any answer, because the voice is our own, even though distantly it might be the voice of our mother or father, living or dead, or it might be the voice of someone we yearn for or have lost. What are you doing in there? I'm painting, I'm writing a poem, I'm doing something you conceivably wouldn't understand. But really I'm only *not* drowning. I can't, for the moment, breathe the same air that propels *you* on your way. I'm submerged. The past is no longer reassuring, it is only relevant in that I can recognize what the light beyond this preoccupation of mine foretells: the sameness of a life that only ever knows subliminal disasters.

But in this moment, sustained by unknowing, as the surface of the deluge erupts intermittently around us, evanescent ideas bobbing absurdly upon the flow like empty silk purses, frustrating in their exquisite lack of purpose, we have found an alternative to any reality (comprised of reassuring convictions) we may have once accepted as viable. Now our work shall be about the business of knowing another reality. And the opening to this reality will be the painting or the poem waiting patiently amidst the fragile atmosphere of tranquility left in the aftermath of the deluge. It was inevitable, we now know, and these things — the indomitable remnants of our passage and our work — shall stand apart from us knowing precisely what we have not known.